MILLIONAIRE MONEY MINDSET

Affirmations, Meditation, & Hypnosis: Using Positive Thinking Psychology to Train Your Mind to Grow Wealth, Think Like the New Rich and Take the Secret Fastlane to Success

DREW MCARTHUR

© Copyright 2019 by Drew McArthur - All rights reserved.

The following book is reproduced below with the goal of providing information that is as accurate and reliable as possible. Regardless, purchasing this book can be seen as consent to the fact that both the publisher and the author of this book are in no way experts on the topics discussed within and that any recommendations or suggestions that are made herein are for entertainment purposes only. Professionals should be consulted as needed prior to undertaking any of the action endorsed herein.

This declaration is deemed fair and valid by both the American Bar Association and the Committee of Publishers Association and is legally binding throughout the United States.

Furthermore, the transmission, duplication or reproduction of any of the following work including specific information will be considered an illegal act irrespective of if it is done electronically or in print. This extends to creating a secondary or tertiary copy of the work or a recorded copy and is only allowed with express written consent from the Publisher. All additional right reserved.

The information in the following pages is broadly considered to be a truthful and accurate account of facts, and as such any inattention, use or misuse of the information in question by the reader will render any resulting actions solely under their purview. There are no scenarios in which the publisher or the original author of this work can be in any fashion deemed liable for any hardship or damages that may befall them after undertaking information described herein.

Additionally, the information in the following pages is intended only for informational purposes and should thus be thought of as universal. As befitting its nature, it is presented without assurance regarding its prolonged validity or interim quality. Trademarks that are mentioned are done without written consent and can in no way be considered an endorsement from the trademark holder.

All by Drew McArthur on Amazon & Audible

Affirmations, Meditation, & Hypnosis For Positivity & A Success Mindset:

Power Of Thought To Create A Millionaire Mind, Manifest Wealth, Abundance, Better Relationships, & Form Positive Habits Now

Rewire Your Brain Affirmations, Meditation, & Hypnosis For Confidence, Motivation, & Discipline:

Increase Focus, Productivity, Willpower, Self Esteem, & Eliminate Distraction & Procrastination Habits

Step-By-Step Motivational Goal Setting Course For Life Mastery:

How To Change Your Brain, Set Your Vision, And Get Everything You Want To Have Your Best Year Ever

Monkey Mind Cure Affirmations, Meditation & Hypnosis:

How to Stop Worrying, Kill Fear, Rewire Your Brain, and Change Your Anxious Thoughts to Start Living a Stress and Anxiety-Free Life

Think Happy Thoughts: Affirmations and Meditation for Positive Thinking, Learned Optimism and a Happy Brain

Unlock the Advantage of the Happiness Habit and Project the Power of Positive Energy

Millionaire Money Mindset: Affirmations, Meditation, & Hypnosis

Using Positive Thinking Psychology to Train Your Mind to Grow Wealth, Think Like the New Rich and Take the Secret Fastlane to Success

Contents

Introduction	ix
Establishing Your Foundation: Habits & Philosophy	1
Attitude & Relationship with Money	11
Taking Accountability & Responsibility	37
Being A Confident Leader	57
Building, Keeping, & Growing Wealth	67
Overcoming Limiting Beliefs	107
Cultivating Abundance In Thought & Reality	115
Success	121
All by Drew McArthur on Amazon & Audible	129

Introduction

What makes the wealthy, wealthy? What makes the successful, successful? And why is it that the rich seem to get richer? And the more successful people become, the more successful they become? It all stems from the mind. Your actions will never go where your thoughts have not already been, and the fact is that wealthy people think differently. The millionaire mindset begins with a positive relationship with money and a positive view of money. It often requires eliminating the negative programming around money that has been put

Introduction

into our heads by our parents, friends, society, and the media....

"Money is the root of all evil."

"Rich people are dishonest and selfish."

"It's bad to want to be rich."

"There's not enough for everyone to be rich."

"Everyone who's rich either got lucky, cheated their way there, or was born that way."

"It's not possible for people like me to be rich."

Thoughts and embedded beliefs like these repel wealth and make it impossible to reach greater financial heights. Wealthy people know this. They know that the desire to be rich is simply the desire to maximize their potential, gain the resources to allow themselves and their loved ones to live their best lives, help those that need it on a large scale in a way only money can do, and provide products and services that are so valuable and helpful that consumers are happy to exchange their money for them. And they know that a healthy desire for money, a positive relationship with money, honest work, and proper stewardship over your finances is the best way to get there.

The road to wealth and success for most is often impeded by a poverty mentality that is shaped by unconscious programs our minds are wired to carry out from the ideas put in our heads a long time ago by outside influences. But a poverty mentality is not just about negative thoughts and beliefs about money. It is about being trapped with an "I can't" attitude. It's a thought process that often blames others for your present circumstances, whether it's your spouse, your boss, the president, or the economy. Poverty is a state of mind, and people who remain in financial poverty are the type of people who always find reasons why they can't, and have an endless supply of excuses for what they would have done, stories about what they should have done, and rants what they could have done if it weren't for some external force outside of themselves that they blame for their shortcomings and unrealized dreams.

Successful people with the millionaire mindset take responsibility and control over themselves, their actions, and their outcomes, which in turn gives them control over their lives. While others talk about doing things, they take action and never blame others or external forces for their circumstances. They don't wait around for luck, the economy to turn around, that perfect business partner to walk into their lives, their bank account to magically double…they change what they don't like and know and believe that they can do so.

They are leaders, who take control and lead themselves, businesses, projects, and other people down the path towards success. They are decisive and like to be in control rather than sitting on the sidelines, because they are confident in their ability to make good decisions with good outcomes.

Whether we like it or not, we are all leaders, it's just a matter of whether we are good leaders or bad leaders. Leadership begins at home, so to be a leader, you need to be a leader of self first. This begins with becoming a master at your time management and owning your productivity. It also means taking pride in your work and bringing excellence to everything you do on every level, as you make your climb to the top, no matter who is or is not looking. People destined for success have good, foundational habits that they apply in their daily lives, whether that means showing up early to a meeting, being the first to volunteer for a task at work, or taking small daily action steps towards their entrepreneurial dreams. It is from these basic habitual actions and your foundational attitude through which everything else flows.

And while successful people make a lot of money, they know that material riches are not the only important type of riches to have. They know that wealth reaches far beyond money alone. Success is about more than just financial success. So they prioritize the people in their lives by balancing their work with family, relationships, recreation, and their personal lives. They are cheerful givers with an attitude of service within their work, and an attitude of charity outside of their work.

Sometimes, it seems that we're doing all the right things and taking all the right actions

Introduction

to move towards our goals, but we still can't see progress or results. Your mindset makes all the difference. Disempowering thoughts can make you feel helpless, and hopeless. And these negative thoughts are often rooted in our subconscious, so we don't even realize the psychological damage we're doing to ourselves. But training your brain to be positive, optimistic, and expect good things to happen to you and for you, can be the difference between seeing success, and not seeing success.

It's time to think big, and stop being plagued and crippled by limiting beliefs. There is limitless potential and unlimited abundance for everyone who desires success and wealth. It is time to join those with the millionaire mindset. Hard work always pays off, and there are unlimited opportunities to create wealth. Anyone and

Introduction

everyone can become successful, including you.

It's time to adopt the thought processes of the rich and use affirmations to drive those thoughts into your subconscious. These affirmations will help you develop the right attitudes and habits for success. Because from new thoughts will spring new actions that will lead you on the right path to wealth in every area of your life.

Affirmations can quite literally rewire your mind, by physically affecting the neural pathways in your brain. Affirmations, when spoken coupled with the feeling one would feel if they honestly believed them to be true, can be extremely powerful tools in improving and changing your life.

This audio contains affirmations in the following categories, in the following order:

Introduction

- Establishing Your Foundation: Habits & Philosophy
- Attitude & Relationship with Money
- Taking Accountability & Responsibility
- Being A Confident Leader
- Building, Keeping, & Growing Wealth
- Overcoming Limiting Beliefs
- Cultivating Abundance In Thought & Reality
- Success

Some sections are a little bit shorter. Some are a longer. So you can select the chapter of your choice based on what you have time for at that given time. Or you can listen straight through all chapters. Because this is designed for audio and continuous listening, there is no conclusion for this audiobook.

Introduction

Now, let's see how you can make the most out of this audio...

You can use this audiobook as affirmations, meditation, or hypnosis. If you choose to use it as affirmations, I suggest that you pick a time and a place where you will feel completely confident speaking each affirmation out loud. Maybe for you, that's your bathroom in front of your mirror before bed every night. Maybe it's your living room when the kids are away at soccer practice. Maybe it's your car on your commute on your way to work. No matter where you choose to recite your affirmations, remember that the whole point of this is to ingrain positive, strong thoughts in your head. So, make sure your body language reflects that also. Depending upon where you are, stand up straight, or sit up straight while you speak each statement aloud. Make sure your shoulders are back and your head is up. The confidence in

Introduction

your body needs to be in alignment with the confidence in your words and thoughts in order for this to work. You cannot speak powerful statements and think positive thoughts, while having a slumped, unconfident, disempowered posture in your body.

If you would like to use this as meditation, before you begin, find a quiet place where you will remain undisturbed for the entire length of the audio. Then, remove all distractions. Turn off your phone, eliminate as much noise as possible, close the door to where ever you are, and alert anyone around you not to disturb you for the next two hours. When you're ready to begin, find a comfortable position, either sitting up or laying down, and be sure to remove all physical tension from your body. Choose a position that is comfortable enough for you to allow the muscles of your body to relax, but that will also ensure that you stay awake. Many people like to sit with their legs crossed and their hands resting palm up or down on their knees. Some people prefer to lay down on their backs, with their arms palms up, by their sides. Choose whichever is best for you. Then, once you are settled into position, you can either choose a spot to look at and drop your eyelids and soften your gaze, or you can close your eyes altogether. Then, begin clearing your mind of all past, present, and future thoughts and worries, and deepen your relaxed state by slowing your breathing to long, deep breaths, fully inhaling, then fully exhaling. When you feel you are adequately relaxed, begin the audio. If you like, you can just listen to the audio and let the words seep into your mind and your consciousness, or you can repeat them in your head during the pauses.

Lastly, if you would like to use this as hypnosis, simply start the audio and let it play when you go to bed, allowing the words to embed themselves into your subconscious as you fall asleep.

It doesn't matter how you choose to use this audio, as all of the methods can be effective for you, and make a noticeable difference in your default state of mind and your future success. The ideal scenario may even be to use a combination of all three. That way, you can not only consciously absorb these thoughts, but you can also simultaneously subconsciously absorb them as well. The most important thing is to be consistent. Whatever you do, make sure you do it every day—even multiple times a day if you have time. You can begin your day with affirmations, and end it with meditation and hypnosis. But just keep doing it. Change will not happen overnight. It will take time to reprogram your mind for success, but I assure you, it will be well worth the effort.

Introduction

Don't worry about looking or sounding weird to other people. Don't worry about what other people may think of you. Whenever you feel strange or uncomfortable about doing this, just remember why you are doing this and think about your goals. If you need help setting goals, I have a program available on Audible that can help you with that task.

I also have several other affirmations audio programs that will help you continue your quest towards habitual positive thinking. So be sure to check out my other titles on Audible and Amazon.

And now, let us begin. Welcome to the next step in becoming a better, happier, more effective version of yourself. Are you ready?

Establishing Your Foundation: Habits & Philosophy

1. I approach each day with excitement and anticipation.
2. I do everything well to the best of my ability, no matter how big or how small.
3. I am joyfully living a life of service for all humankind.
4. I enjoy being responsible for my own outcomes.
5. I am strong enough to meet any challenge, no matter how difficult it first appears.

6. I focus on what is important and create my own reality.
7. I create my circumstances, not the other way around.
8. I have the strength and talent to complete any task I am given with excellence.
9. I am surrounded by successful people who inspire me.
10. I attract people who are productive and who help me reach my goals.
11. I get any task assigned to be done easily and before others.
12. I hold a leadership role in my life, in my work, and in my home, and I handle it well.
13. I always accept responsibility and take action to right my mistakes.
14. I am sincere and honest in my actions.
15. I possess integrity and my morals

and ethics are the backbone of everything I do.
16. I accept holding positions of authority, and I also accept the responsibility that goes along with it.
17. I am an independent thinker and I make my own decisions.
18. I do what is right for me regardless of what others think or do.
19. I work hard but I always take the time for needed rest and recuperation.
20. I am persistent and will always keep moving forward.
21. There is always a way around any obstacle.
22. I always find a way to use obstacles for my benefit.
23. I have a habit of doing my hardest tasks first to ease my path to success later.

24. Each day, I create value for others in my work and in my personal life.
25. I work hard because I know it will always be worth it in the end.
26. As long as I do my part, I am always progressing and moving forward even when it doesn't feel like it.
27. Even though I work hard, it feels effortless and fun to me.
28. My personal life gets just as much attention from me as my professional life.
29. The work I put in allows my family to live a better life.
30. I am always on time because I respect the value of my time and other people's time.
31. I am organized and effective in everything I do.
32. I control my circumstances, not the other way around.

33. I ensure that I get things done early and always make deadlines.
34. I express gratitude and praise for the contributions of others.
35. I get things done now instead of putting them off for later.
36. There truly is no time like the present.
37. I am dedicated to making my life the best it can be in every area.
38. I enjoy my rewards after I've completed my work.
39. I stay motivated no matter what task I have before me.
40. I put what seem like obstacles into proper perspective and proportion.
41. I am proactive and take initiative.
42. I always make my voice heard because I know what I have to say is valuable.
43. I am confident and motivated.
44. I am in good health and full of energy.

45. I am a creative vessel constantly flowing with new, great ideas.
46. I have the power to create and build limitless abundance.
47. I am responsible with my money and finances.
48. I make decisions for the long term, not the short term.
49. Mistakes made are only lessons to be learned.
50. I grow and improve from situations that seem like failure.
51. I accept praise and credit only when I deserve it and I also openly give praise and credit to others.
52. I have a win/win attitude and look for ways for everyone to benefit from every situation.
53. I am efficient and believe in my ability to get things done quickly and well.
54. I am strong enough to power my way through adversity.

55. I face the unknown with confidence and strength.
56. I create, build upon, and maximize my momentum.
57. I am unstoppable and will attain anything I put my mind to.
58. I seek ways to get out of my comfort zone because that is how I grow.
59. I get things done in a short amount of time without sacrificing quality.
60. I recognize when things are too big to go it alone and I collaborate well with others.
61. I am empathetic and I make hearing others more important than making myself heard.
62. I strive to understand others first in conversation and make listening a priority.
63. I take full responsibility and accountability for everything that happens in my life.

64. Although I work hard, I always seek balance and do fun and new things.
65. I am not only rich financially, but I have rich relationships with friends and family.
66. I have complete control over my time and energy.
67. I am willing to put in the work to create success, not just the talk.
68. I am focused and do not let anything distract me from my work.
69. The reality I experience tomorrow, I am creating right now, today.
70. I am a happy person who spreads my happiness to others.
71. I approach obstacles and challenges with calmness, confidence, and strength.
72. I am in perfect health, and full of the energy I need to create and live my best life.

73. I listen to my feelings and trust my own intuition.
74. I always keep my promises and live up to my commitments.
75. I am in control of what happens in my life, not society, government, or economy.
76. Success comes to me effortlessly.
77. I focus only on what's important.
78. I have faith in my future because I know that I create it.
79. I desire prosperity for the benefit of myself and others, and I attract it to me.
80. I am constantly increasing my value to myself, my profession, and other people.
81. I am deeply satisfied with my work and contribution.
82. I determine my outcomes, not external circumstances.

Attitude & Relationship with Money

1. I always have more than enough money to meet my needs.
2. I pay myself first, but I always share my money to help others who need help.
3. I deserve to be wealthy.
4. My wealth grows in proportion to the service I provide others.
5. My wealth grows in proportion to the value I provide others.
6. I can afford anything and everything my heart desires.

7. I am drawing money toward me all the time.
8. I have the power to create all the wealth my family needs.
9. I deserve financial abundance and material prosperity.
10. I own money, but money does not own me.
11. I find it easy to attract money into my life.
12. I choose to be rich and powerful, but to use it to make a positive impact in the lives of others.
13. I know that my wealth is not just for me, but for the betterment of others as well.
14. The world is full of riches and I know that I will get my share.
15. I attract money wherever I go and no matter what I am doing.
16. I love money and feel the good that comes from it.
17. I am the one who has complete

control over the amount of money I have in my life.
18. I choose to be wealthy and recognize that life is magnificent.
19. Money is good when it is used for good.
20. I am increasing my wealth, which gives me the power to increase my freedom.
21. I use money to improve the lives of myself and my family.
22. I use money to open new doors to more success.
23. Money is a tool that I can use to create my best life.
24. Money is a tool that I can use to support others in living their best life.
25. Having or wanting money is nothing to feel guilt or shame over.
26. Money is a seed, which when planted properly, will grow.
27. I freely invest money into my

business, knowing that I will always make a significant return.
28. I freely invest money into myself, knowing that I will always make a significant return.
29. I am responsible with my money, and I always find ways to make it grow.
30. I use and invest my money responsibly.
31. I enjoy the power that comes from financial independence.
32. I am always growing my wealth, no matter the state of the economy.
33. I am always growing my wealth, no matter the political climate.
34. I am always thinking of new ways to make money.
35. I act on my ideas that create prosperity.
36. My wealth is growing every single day.

37. I am just as capable of creating, growing, and maintaining wealth as anyone else.
38. It is possible for money to come and flow to me easily.
39. There is no limit to the amount of wealth I can create.
40. I choose to share my wealth with others.
41. I find it easy to make money and make more and more with each passing day.
42. I attract wealth to me from all corners of the world.
43. I am strong enough to grow wealth despite my upbringing.
44. I have a positive mental attitude around money.
45. I have a healthy relationship with money.
46. I am in control of money, not the other way around.

47. I am unstoppable when it comes to generating massive wealth.
48. I enjoy making money.
49. My income is always effortlessly increasing.
50. I don't always have to work for money, I make my money work for me.
51. I put my money to work in profitable investments.
52. I make passive income from my money.
53. While I sleep and play, my money is still working and growing for me.
54. I can make lots of money without trading my time for it.
55. The actions I do today will result in more wealth, prosperity, and abundance.
56. I feel good, joyous, and positive when it comes to money.
57. Money is not the only thing that

brings me happiness and fulfilment.
58. It is okay to feel happy and excited about making money.
59. It is okay to be wealthy.
60. It is my right to be rich.
61. My bank account continues to grow more than I ever thought possible.
62. I use the money I have to make more money.
63. I have all the wealth I could ever need or want.
64. I am surrounded by wealth and abundance.
65. My relationships are just as rich as my bank account.
66. I am always receiving wealth because I am willing to ask for it.
67. I am always receiving wealth because I am willing to work for it.
68. My inputs result in increase.

69. Having money gives me options, which is a good thing.
70. Wealth allows me to choose what I want for my life, while poverty would make my choices for me.
71. I am a magnet for money and prosperity.
72. I have so much wealth I can share it with others effortlessly.
73. I can create and produce whatever amount of money I need at will.
74. I have the money I want and need because I ask for the money I want and need.
75. I am surrounded by opportunities to make more money.
76. I already have the ideas I need to make more money, I just need to act on them.
77. The world has all the money I could ever want.
78. I earn my money, fair and square.

79. I can make a lot of money and still be a good person.
80. I have my own positive opinions of money despite the opinions of others from my past.
81. I have my own positive relationship to money despite others from my past.
82. I can be both rich and humble.
83. I can be both rich and kind.
84. I can be both rich and loving.
85. I can be both rich and generous.
86. I can be both rich and honest.
87. I provide value and service to others in my work, which results in more money and wealth for me.
88. I have the capability to be responsible with my wealth.
89. I have the capability to grow my wealth.
90. As my professional service and contribution grow, as does my bank account.

91. I never take more in monetary value from others than value I provide them.
92. I deserve the wealth that I am receiving.
93. Whether it take a short or a long time to grow my wealth, I am as patient as I need to be.
94. Money is drawn to me and I accept it with gratitude.
95. I respect money and recognize it as a tool that provides liberty, prosperity, and freedom.
96. Money gives me opportunities in life to do, have, and become things that most can only dream of.
97. I enjoy money, wealth, and prosperity.
98. I am comfortable with having wealth and riches.
99. I deserve financial independence and financial abundance.

100. If I want to increase my income, I must increase my standards.
101. In order for my money to grow, I must grow.
102. I am always able to figure out ways to make money.
103. I am free of debt.
104. Anything I want, I can pay for in full.
105. I surround myself with people who are financially responsible.
106. I have an abundance of money that can help me handle any life situation that comes up.
107. I am master over my money, not the other way around.
108. I will always be wealthy.
109. Everyone deserves to have money to live their best life, and I will take my share without guilt.
110. I see a way to make money from new ideas every day.

111. I am comfortable with the money that hard work brings.
112. I have so much money that I always feel financially secure.
113. Money is good because it brings security to my family.
114. Money is good because it makes it easier for me to help others.
115. My mind is clear and calm because my financial needs are taken care of.
116. Money gives me the ability to do what I want to do, not just what I have to do.
117. Money is a ticket that allows me to do whatever I want in life.
118. Being wealthy allows me to make decisions based on growth and desire, not desperation and restriction.
119. The state of the economy has no bearing on the amount of money I make.

120. I thrive in economic times where others panic.
121. There are opportunities all around me to grow wealth.
122. Money is generously given to me and I generously give it to others.
123. I trust that I will always have more than enough money to meet my needs.
124. I love the feeling I get when I receive money well-earned.
125. I am thankful and appreciative when I receive money because I know that others don't always have it.
126. I find it easy to meet my financial goals.
127. My financial security makes it possible for me to help others.
128. My money allows me to better support my health.
129. Every single day, the amount of money I have grows.

130. I feel light and happy when I think about money.
131. The thing I love the most about money is how it enables me to change the world.
132. The stronger I am the more money I attract.
133. I deserve any amount of money I could wish for.
134. I have all the money I could possibly dream of.
135. I am proud and deserving of the wealth and money I have earned.
136. My wealthy mindset enables me to create money.
137. I admire the wealthy and successful and strive to be more like them.
138. I learn from rich and successful people who teach me about wealth generation.
139. My heart is open to receiving wealth, money, and prosperity.

140. I am getting closer and closer to my financial goals every day.
141. I allow and welcome wealth and money to enter into my life.
142. Financial increase is constant and inevitable for me.
143. I am comfortable looking at my bank account and seeing it grow.
144. I can earn as much money as I want and need.
145. Being wealthy and prosperous is my natural state of being.
146. I set financial goals and always achieve them faster than I thought I would.
147. Money can help buy happiness because it buys opportunity and freedom of choice.
148. I give myself permission to be rich.
149. It's okay for me to maximize my potential by making as much money as I possibly can.

150. I do the world a favor by making as much money as I possibly can.
151. I do my loved ones a favor by making as much money as I possibly can.
152. I do myself a favor by making as much money as I possibly can.
153. The more money I make, the more money I can give.
154. The more money I make, the more money I give.
155. My ability to grow wealth is inspiring to others.
156. Pursuing wealth makes me a better person because I have to grow as a person for my money to grow.
157. Money is good and helps others.
158. I am responsible with my money, but I also enjoy it.
159. I gladly allow wealth to enter my life.

160. I can and will become rich, solely because I choose to.
161. I spend money without guilt or shame.
162. I love spending money on others to help them get what they need and desire.
163. I deserve all the money I have and even more.
164. I deserve all the money that is coming to me, and even more.
165. I give myself permission to openly receive all the money that is coming to me.
166. I feel good about money and enjoy it.
167. My heart is completely open to abundance and prosperity.
168. Money flows into my life without me asking for it because I am a magnet for money.
169. I am grateful for the money that

keeps flowing into my life and I will use it for good.
170. I effortlessly attract money into my life through the service that I provide others.
171. I earn my money and my wealth because I make myself a valuable asset to the world.
172. I enjoy investing and love using my money to grow more money.
173. I take calculated financial risks because I am confident I can make them pay off.
174. In my professional life, I fulfill the needs of others in a moral way, and receive money in return.
175. The abundance I have makes me feel light and stress free.
176. I believe I have the ability to earn as much money as I desire.
177. I am mentally strong, so I can earn money in any way that I set out to.

178. I am resourceful, so I can earn money in any way that I set out to.
179. Every single day, I wake up with more money than I had the day before.
180. Every day, my income and my professional success are growing.
181. Attaining financial prosperity is my right and responsibility.
182. It is easy for me to manifest wealth.
183. I help others get the money they desire and deserve because there is plenty for everyone to succeed.
184. I admire honest, wealthy people and value the positive example they provide.
185. I learn from others how to increase my own wealth.
186. I am financially rewarded in proportion to the quality of work I do.

187. My mind and conscience are at ease when I spend money.
188. My mind and conscience are at ease when I grow money.
189. I can boldly say that I love making money.
190. I can boldly say that I love having money.
191. I can boldly say that I love spending money.
192. I can boldly say that I love saving money.
193. I can boldly say that I love growing money.
194. I am comfortable with spending and enjoying my money because I know more is always coming to me.
195. Money is a resource that is always renewing for me.
196. It is okay for me to spend money on the things I want.

197. It is okay for me to spend money on others.
198. I save and invest out of responsibility not fear, because I know more is always coming to me.
199. I always exceed my financial goals and make more money than I want.
200. I grow wealth in every type of economic or political climate.
201. The world is full of money-making opportunities and I always seize them.
202. I can afford to spend lots of money on personal care because of my wealth.
203. I use my money to create the best life for myself and others.
204. Generating wealth is on auto pilot for me.
205. My mind is always thinking of new ways to make money.

206. I love money and wealth.
207. I celebrate being able to buy a wonderful home for myself and my family.
208. I enjoy my financial blessings.
209. There is not ceiling on the amount of money I can make.
210. I use money to learn more and educate myself, to increase my value to others.
211. I have more than enough money and share my overflow with others.
212. I am a positive example for others to embrace money and the freedom it provides.
213. I love to give money away because I can easily create more.
214. I could regenerate my wealth from scratch if I had to.
215. I have a wealth mindset and have a positive attitude about money.

216. I find it easy to make money on demand.
217. The ability to help others motivates me to grow my wealth even more.
218. I am rich, wealth, and prosperous.
219. My investments always yield long term profits.
220. I am growing richer by the day.
221. The work I put in today will pay off financially tomorrow.
222. I am skilled in creating and generating money.
223. I can create money-making opportunities for myself and for others.
224. I share money making opportunities with others because there is more than enough money to go around.
225. I am always discovering new money-making opportunities.
226. I have the ability to create my own

money no matter what is happening around me.
227. I have the ability to create my own money no matter who is around me.
228. It is okay for money to make me feel happy.
229. My subconscious acts in alignment with my conscious efforts to earn and grow wealth.
230. I have the power to create money through my mind and can do so whenever I need to.
231. I have the power to attract money into my life and increase prosperity.
232. I have the power to forever defeat debt and poverty.
233. I feel joy and satisfaction when I have the money to spend on things I want and need.
234. Wealth is the natural state of my life.

235. Having lots of money is the natural state of my life.
236. With every new day, I will claim the money-making opportunities it brings.
237. I choose to feel good about money, and the prosperity and security it can bring.
238. I choose to feel good about money, and the mental peace it can bring.
239. I love all the money I earn and every dollar in my bank account.
240. I cultivate positive feelings about money every day.
241. Money supports my life and dreams in every possible way.
242. I choose to let go of negative feelings I have about money and wealth.
243. I choose to let go of negative perceptions I have about money that I got from other people.

244. I use my leadership abilities and intelligence to attract money.
245. To receive money in the future I will render services to others expecting nothing in return.
246. I use seed money to plant new riches to be realized in the future.
247. I donate to worthy causes out of the goodness of my heart.
248. I feel myself becoming more and more wealthy each passing day.
249. Pursing financial goals is a worthy pursuit.
250. I make sound financial decisions.
251. I have gratitude for all the wealth and money I have received, created, and built.
252. I make lots of money and deserve every dollar of it.
253. I give away money every month to help realize other people's dreams and make the world a better place.

Taking Accountability & Responsibility

1. I am here today as a result of the actions I took yesterday.
2. If I don't like something in my life, I will change it.
3. Things only change when my actions change.
4. Things only change when my attitude changes.
5. I am responsible for all results that happen as a result of my actions.
6. I am in control of my thoughts and I choose to think positively.
7. I do what I need to do to make

sure I am mentally free and clear enough to create success.
8. I take a step each day to grow wealth tomorrow.
9. The problems in my life are my fault and not the fault of others.
10. There is no such thing as luck, I create my own fortune.
11. My financial success depends on my own actions, not on the economy.
12. My financial success depends on my own actions, not on the political climate.
13. My financial success depends on my own actions, not my upbringing.
14. My financial success depends on my own actions, not others around me.
15. I control my own financial future and I choose prosperity.

16. I create my own reality with my own thoughts.
17. I can change the circumstances around me with right thought and action.
18. I think I can, I know I can, and I will.
19. I have complete control over my destiny.
20. I will do whatever it takes within moral and ethical reason to succeed.
21. When I do something wrong, I take action to make it right.
22. Talk is cheap; I grow my success by action and results.
23. I accept each new challenge as an opportunity for growth.
24. I take responsibility for who I am today.
25. I accept that I have created the bad as well as the good in my life.
26. If I don't like the way my life is

going, it is my responsibility to do something about it.
27. I am responsible for changing my own life; nobody else can do it for me.
28. Takers lose and givers win. I choose to be a giver.
29. My success in every area of my life is determined by my own actions.
30. When I provide value to others, I receive money and financial success in return.
31. I am responsible for how I perceive adversity.
32. I am responsible for how I respond to adversity.
33. I am in control of my reactions to situations around me.
34. I am in control of my habits and impulses.
35. I have the ability to create new good habits, and get rid of bad old ones.

36. I am in control of my mood and temper and always find a positive way to react to any situation.
37. I alone am responsible for my happiness.
38. I am responsible for my career situation and will change it if I don't like it.
39. I accept that everything I did before has lead me to the point where I am today.
40. For better or worse, I am the sum total of all of my choices.
41. If I want my life to be better, I have to make better decisions.
42. My own health is in my control.
43. I am in control of how much money flows into my life.
44. I accept responsibility for any failures in my life.
45. I learn from each apparent failure in my life.
46. I choose to reframe what seems

like failure as a lesson I will use to succeed next time.
47. I am responsible for the income that I generate.
48. No matter the outcome of my life, I either created it or allowed it.
49. No matter my circumstances, I have the ability to turn my life around.
50. I am responsible for using my unique gifts and talents to the maximum extent possible.
51. I take responsibility to learn the skills and gain the education I need to achieve success.
52. I take responsibility for listening to others when they offer constructive criticism.
53. I am responsible for my current financial situation and will take specific actions to change it if I am not happy about it.
54. I am responsible for the words

that come out of my mouth that can impact my success in work or in business.

55. I am responsible for the quality of the thoughts in my head.
56. The problems I perceive in my life are all fixable.
57. I adopt a wealth mentality to ensure my financial success.
58. I am in charge of my own life and do not look to others for excuses.
59. I am responsible for my past.
60. I am responsible for my present.
61. I am responsible for my future.
62. I will do what needs to be done to create my best future possible.
63. I am in complete control of how I respond to whatever happens to me.
64. I have the power to turn any negative into a positive.
65. I have the power to perceive any negative as a positive.

66. The life that I am leading is the life that I chose through my actions.
67. It is my responsibility to take action to correct any mistakes that I have made.
68. I take responsibility for seeing the good in other people.
69. I choose to speak kindly about others.
70. I take responsibility for the price I must pay for success.
71. If there is a better way to do something, I realize I must discover this for myself.
72. I own my mistakes and take action to correct them.
73. I accept responsibility for my physical health and recognize that I alone can change it.
74. I accept responsibility for the status of my relationships and recognize that I alone can change them.

75. I am responsible for my feelings.
76. I am in control of my emotions.
77. I take action to maintain mental strength and clarity.
78. I own my energy.
79. I am responsible for where I am in my life, not my friends.
80. I am responsible for where I am in my life, not my family.
81. I am responsible for where I am in my life, not my government.
82. I am responsible for where I am in my life, not my boss.
83. I point the finger at myself first, not others.
84. I always find a way to make it happen.
85. I make results, not excuses.
86. Nothing holds me back from achieving success.
87. No one holds me back from achieving success.
88. Every single day I take at least one

step to become more responsible over my own life.
89. I choose my response in the face of a challenge.
90. I cannot control other people and how they perceive me, but I can put my best foot forward at all times.
91. I am responsible for always being prepared.
92. I am responsible for saving money for financial emergencies.
93. I am responsible for my own fate and do not depend on anyone else to keep my ship afloat.
94. I am responsible for the people I allow into my life.
95. No one is coming to save me, I have to better my own life if I want it to be better.
96. I take full responsibility for the person I become tomorrow as a

result of the actions I am taking today.
97. I choose to better my surroundings with right thought and action.
98. I live a life of no excuses and no regrets.
99. I am not responsible for the circumstances I was born into, but I am responsible for every action I've taken since.
100. I always have a choice.
101. My past negative experiences have no bearing on my future success.
102. I am strong and in complete control of my own destiny.
103. I am a shot taker and a way maker.
104. I depend only on myself for my financial success.
105. Anything I want, I can create.
106. I confront challenges head on.
107. Past failures and struggles are a

result of my attitude, which I take full responsibility for now.
108. Past failures and struggles are a result of my actions, which I take full responsibility for now.
109. I recognize that if my life isn't going right, I am the one who needs to change.
110. Whenever I don't like the way I feel, I change the behaviors that cause those feelings.
111. I choose to adopt a positive attitude each and every single day.
112. I embrace change as an opportunity for growth.
113. I always see the positive in everything that happens.
114. I always see the positive in every person I cross paths with.
115. The problems in my life are all temporary and easier to overcome than I think.

116. I am the only one who can change how I feel inside.
117. I do not compare myself to others.
118. I understand that I am running my own race.
119. I know that I can have anything I want, so I live a life free of envy.
120. I know that I can have anything I work for, so I live a life free of jealousy.
121. I am in control of my emotions, and I choose to live free of resentment.
122. I take responsibility for remaining humble and true to myself as my wealth increases.
123. I replace scattered thinking with specific goals to improve my life.
124. I refuse to engage in self-pity.
125. I do not manipulate others by trying to get them to feel pity for me.

126. I am always calm and relaxed under pressure.
127. I am flexible and resourceful when things don't go my way.
128. I am social and friendly and take initiative in social situations.
129. I have a healthy social life that helps keep my mind on positive things.
130. I fill each of my days with joy and laughter.
131. I replace thoughts of self-pity with concern for others.
132. I am responsible for providing the service to others that leads to my own wealth.
133. There is always money to be made and I will not let external circumstances control my fate.
134. I replace impatience with persistence and hard work.
135. I am honest, and people are honest with me.

136. I take action to ensure that I am always full of energy and vitality.
137. I wake up each day feeling optimism, hope, and love.
138. I can and will change any situation that I don't like.
139. I am always open to change and embrace it.
140. I accept help from others when I need it.
141. I seek answers when I don't already know them.
142. I am open to the idea that someone else may know more than me.
143. I am open to the idea that someone else may know better than me.
144. I am responsible for making every moment of every day fulfilling.
145. I move forward past fear when it arises.
146. I am confident and optimistic about my future.

147. I am passionate about my life, present and future.
148. I realize that every decision I've made up to this point has led me to where I am right now.
149. I keep my mind fixed on positive and uplifting things.
150. I guard my mind and only allow positive thoughts and images to enter it.
151. It can be done, and I can do it.
152. I don't let anything stop me from moving towards my goals.
153. What I see in my mind, I create in my life, so I take full responsibility for my life vision.
154. When I feel frustration, I calmly find a way forward.
155. I seek help and support when I need it.
156. I offer help and support when I am able to.
157. I am reliable and dependable.

158. I keep my promises to others.
159. I take my commitments seriously.
160. I own my reputation and every part I played in creating it.
161. I am responsible for keeping my mind in a happy state.
162. What I perceive to be problems in my life can all be used to my advantage.
163. Anything that is wrong, I can make right.
164. There are no limits on what I can achieve.
165. I am a good steward of my finances.
166. I am responsible for responsible spending.
167. I always live within my financial means.
168. I am deliberate about filling my time with activities that push me forward.

169. I am deliberate about filling my time with activities that I enjoy.
170. I am intentional about spending my time with positive people that I love.
171. I alone control my attitude about money, success, and prosperity.
172. Instead of living on auto-pilot, I take direct control over my outcomes.
173. I am in charge of my attitude, and I choose a cheerful one.
174. I choose to seek and find opportunities instead of obstacles.
175. I seek joy, therefore I find joy.
176. I seek love, therefore I find love.
177. I seek success, therefore I find success.
178. I am willing to put my pride aside to do what it takes to succeed.
179. I am responsible for acting with maximum efficiency and efficacy.

180. It is up to me to improve my skills as needed.
181. My financial success is not controlled by big corporations or big government.
182. I am willing to pay the short-term price for long-term success.
183. I accept the consequences for all of my actions.
184. I am willing to be the first to extend a helping hand.
185. I always pay it forward.
186. I make the first move, and don't wait for others to.
187. I am strong enough to overcome any and every obstacle I face with grace.

Being A Confident Leader

1. I confidently take control of every situation in my life.
2. I can count on myself and I can be counted on by others.
3. I take charge of every situation that comes in front of me.
4. As a leader, I accept responsibility for the direction of my own life.
5. I choose my path.
6. I make the plans I need to forge ahead in my life.
7. I lead and inspire others by showing results in my own life.

8. I judge myself by the results I create.
9. I am creative and resourceful.
10. I find solutions to every problem.
11. I am intuitive and trust myself to figure out the best way forward.
12. As a leader, I am guided by a cause that is greater than me.
13. I help others to fulfill their potential.
14. I respond confidently when called upon to act as a leader.
15. I am organized and able to make things happen.
16. I accept responsibility for my decisions.
17. I take action towards making change right now.
18. I am willing and able to guide others.
19. I accept, love, and trust myself.
20. I stare failure in the face and become stronger because of it.

21. I take responsibility for all outcomes, good, or bad.
22. I trust myself to make good decisions.
23. I believe in my ability to make good plans.
24. I set good examples in all my personal relationships.
25. I own both my natural strengths and weaknesses.
26. I set definite goals as part of my role as a leader.
27. I take deliberate action towards my goals as part of my role as a leader.
28. I take consistent action towards my goals as part of my role as a leader.
29. I show people by my example how to be a doer.
30. I approach all challenges with faith and enthusiasm.

31. I make the right choices when faced with challenging decisions.
32. People seek me out for advice because of my mental strength and wisdom.
33. I devote time to continually study and learn so I can be an educated leader.
34. People trust my leadership because I make thoughtful decisions.
35. I am able to organize my thoughts clearly and don't let emotion cloud my decision making.
36. I am a leader who is fair to those who follow me.
37. I blame myself, not those who follow me, for mistakes.
38. I am a take charge kind of person.
39. I am able to challenge others to do better than they thought possible.
40. I inspire others to push past their perceived personal limits.

41. I have the wisdom to know when it's time to keep going and when it's time to change course.
42. I direct all my resources towards meeting my goals.
43. People know they can count on me in tough times.
44. I can create calm from chaos.
45. I can create order from disaster.
46. I can create faith from fear.
47. I can persuade people through calmness and reason.
48. I speak in front of others with confidence.
49. I speak up for what I know is right.
50. I boldly and confidently exert my opinion.
51. I talk to strangers with ease and confidence.
52. I always do my best in everything I do whether I get credit or not.
53. I am willing to do more than is

asked of me, even when no one is looking.
54. I inspire people to action.
55. It is easy for me to speak up for myself and for others who can't speak up for themselves.
56. I am not afraid to let my opinions be known.
57. I act with confidence and decisiveness.
58. I trust that the decisions I make are the right ones to move forward.
59. I put in work each day to improve my leadership skills.
60. I keep it together in a crisis and enjoy the extra challenge it brings.
61. I get results when called upon to act.
62. I act even when not called upon to act.
63. I take initiative whether asked to or not.

64. I recognize that my actions don't only affect me, but impact the lives of those I lead.
65. I take my leadership positions at work and home seriously.
66. I seek out opportunity rather than waiting for it to come to me.
67. I have the courage to make decisions.
68. I am decisive and calm and trust the decisions that I make.
69. I pursue goals that help others and raise the status of all those I lead.
70. My actions are always ethical and moral in pursuit of my goals.
71. I think win/win and always consider the needs of others.
72. I lead by my positive example, which naturally draws people towards me.
73. My number one goal in leadership is to elevate those below me.
74. I always keep my eye on the big

picture and maintain sight of my goals.
75. I am a great role model because I walk the walk and talk the talk.
76. I find it easy to maintain my focus on what lies ahead.
77. I am resilient, and always come up with alternative solutions if one way does not work.
78. I am a natural leader that others look to for inspiration and guidance.
79. I have the ability to draw out the best in others.
80. I am great at creating systems and order to help get things done easier.
81. I am great at creating excitement and enthusiasm in others.
82. I take reasonable, calculated risks without being reckless.
83. I ensure that the pursuit of my

goals is beneficial to those around me.

84. I am a results oriented person.
85. I help others feel the joy of achievement.
86. I am persistent, but recognize when something isn't working, and I am not afraid to change direction.
87. I conquer my fears and my failures and do not let setbacks deter me from reaching my goals.
88. I understand how to get things done most effectively and efficiently.
89. I communicate clearly and confidently with others.
90. I am able to resolve disputes so that everyone is satisfied.
91. I push others to be and do their best without making unreasonable demands.
92. I always respect and honor those

who follow me and seek my guidance.
93. No goal is worth the sacrifice of my fundamental beliefs and morals.
94. I motivate others to be the best they can be.
95. I listen to myself and my intuition to know how to guide others.
96. I provide strength and direction to myself and others.

Building, Keeping, & Growing Wealth

1. I have unlimited income potential.
2. I have multiple streams of income.
3. I make passive income as a result of the wise investment decisions I make.
4. I am creative, and I use my creativity to solve people's problems, generating wealth.
5. I act on my creative ideas and turn them into wealth.
6. I know that the only way to true wealth is to not trade my time for money.

7. I know that the only way to true wealth is providing value to the marketplace.
8. I know that the only way to true wealth is to sell valuable products and services.
9. I know that the only way to true wealth is to have my own business.
10. I love my business because it puts me in total control of my income.
11. I sell valuable products and services that improve people's lives.
12. Selling is good because it helps people to solve their problems.
13. Selling is good because it provides unlimited income potential for me.
14. My business allows me to choose what I do with my time.
15. I have financial security because I constantly have money coming in from multiple sources.

16. I leverage my time and the time of others to multiply my productivity.
17. I know there is only so much time in the day, so I have a team of people working towards my goals.
18. I have a finite amount of energy, so I use the help of others to get things done.
19. Wealth comes to me daily through various sources.
20. I can create wealth whenever I want or need to.
21. I have wealth that will take care of my family for generations.
22. I am a magnet for prosperity.
23. All of my efforts result in income.
24. I deserve all the money that I earn.
25. My goals are in alignment with the creation of wealth and prosperity.
26. My mind is in alignment with the creation of wealth and prosperity.
27. My spirit is in alignment with the creation of wealth and prosperity.

28. My actions are in alignment with the creation of wealth and prosperity.
29. The more I get, the more I give.
30. The richer I get, the richer I make others.
31. I will improve the service I provide to humankind every single day.
32. I am determined to provide the best product or service that I possibly can.
33. I invest money back into my business to constantly grow it.
34. I invest money back into my business to constantly improve it.
35. My bank account is filled with money and always growing.
36. I can create wealth and money on command, by providing or improving the service I provide to others.

37. I fulfill the needs of others and generate wealth in the process.
38. I allow myself to receive as much wealth as I deserve, which is unlimited.
39. I create prosperity and share it with others.
40. Nothing will stop me from creating as much wealth as possible.
41. The more I give, the more I seem to get.
42. It is my joy to share my wealth.
43. Sharing my money makes it multiply.
44. I am grateful for the freedom that my business affords me.
45. Wealth is a state of mind, so even if restarting from nothing, I can always rebuild it.
46. I do not hoard money, because through its use, I achieve prosperity and liberty.

47. I use my talents to serve others and receive unlimited wealth in return.
48. I satisfy greater needs of the people, and bring greater wealth into my life in return.
49. I generate wealth by helping people get what they want.
50. I expect to be paid in proportion to the service that I provide others, and I will gladly provide that service.
51. My business allows me to live my ultimate lifestyle.
52. I live my life with a win-win philosophy, and generate wealth in a way that both I and my customers benefit.
53. I only increase my prices when I increase the quality or value of the product or service I provide.
54. I always bring my absolute best to whatever I do.

55. Every single task or position deserves my best and that is what I bring.
56. I am open to receiving as much wealth as I am blessed with.
57. There is an infinite amount of wealth to go around.
58. I am only in competition with myself, to do better than I did yesterday.
59. I trust that my hard work will always pay off some way, some day.
60. I am grateful for every person who plays a role in making my dreams a reality.
61. I treat everyone with respect who helps contribute to the realization of my vision.
62. I am diligent and responsible with my income no matter what level it is right now.

63. I save and invest my money at all times, at all income levels.
64. I have no limits for my life and wealth.
65. I know that real wealth exists in the mind and those who have it can create it with ease even if all their money is taken from them.
66. I can create material wealth without limit.
67. Despite my financial success, I always have time and energy for my most cherished relationships and hobbies.
68. I have the knowledge to create real wealth at any time that I want.
69. I give back with abundance in amazing ways, and it returns to me ten-fold.
70. I have an entrepreneurial mindset and live independently on my own terms.
71. I am creative and create wealth

and prosperity through the creative process.
72. I have the ability to profitably monetize all of my ideas.
73. I am wealthy because I turn the ideas in my head into action.
74. I am always wealthy because wealth is a state of mind.
75. I can create money at will because my abundance lies in my creativity.
76. My business allows me to live a life of my choosing.
77. I only compete with myself in improving my own products and services.
78. Every single day is an opportunity to serve others and create wealth in the process.
79. Wealth flows into my life continuously and effortlessly.
80. I have the wisdom to make

profitable investments with my money.
81. Serving others through charity requires wealth, and I generate wealth to help the unfortunate.
82. We all have the right and ability to be wealthy; we just have to ask for it.
83. I speak up and make my needs and desires known, so I get them.
84. No matter what career, profession, or business I choose, I will rise to the top and be prosperous.
85. There are no limits to abundance, and everyone can be wealthy if they choose.
86. I choose to be wealthy and will provide service to others in return.
87. Money can be used for good or for evil and I choose to use it for good.
88. More money just makes you more of what you already are, and I am already kind and generous.

89. I deserve the money I receive because I serve others with love and without hesitation.
90. I deserve whatever I put in the work to earn.
91. The more money I make, the better because the more I can help myself and others.
92. As I grow myself on my personal development journey, my bank account grows.
93. Wealth is not a thing, it's a mindset, and I have the mindset of wealth, which can never be taken away from me.
94. I can grow wealth at any time and place, and the amount of my choosing.
95. I am proud of being rich.
96. I love being rich, and I use my riches to help others.
97. I am always attracting huge amounts of money into my life.

98. I always have an abundance of money because I have an abundance mindset.
99. I always have enough money to meet and exceed my personal financial obligations.
100. I will not be stopped in my quest to shamelessly create as much money as I want.
101. Gaining wealth is a good thing that benefits me and benefits others.
102. Being wealthy allows me to help those in need on a massive scale.
103. I will move past any obstacle that prevents me from earning as much wealth as possible.
104. I attract people into my life that help me reach my goals of wealth, prosperity, and success.
105. It's okay to value money and to want more of it.

106. I expect to grow with each new project I embark upon.
107. I constantly expect bigger and better things in my life.
108. The system is rigged in my favor and the world wants me to be rich.
109. I seize opportunities that come my way with both hands.
110. I use the wealth I generate to generate even more wealth for me.
111. I give myself permission to become rich and successful in every area of life.
112. Constant growth requires constant change, and I am willing to pay that price.
113. How rich I am inside directly correlates to how rich I am outside.
114. My capacity to grow and expand in every way is unlimited.
115. Through wealth, I create

abundance, and through abundance, I create freedom.

116. I freely share the knowledge of how to become wealthy with others.
117. I accept money into my life because I deserve it.
118. I enjoy all life has to offer, including prosperity and wealth.
119. I already have all the tools I need to create wealth in abundance.
120. I feel safe and secure knowing that I can always create unlimited amounts of money.
121. I can create unlimited prosperity and the choice to do so is mine.
122. I am grateful for the talents and traits I have that allow me to build unlimited amounts of wealth.
123. I am so grateful to be able to provide for my family because of my wealth.
124. No person, thing, circumstance, or

obstacle will ever stop me from achieving my goal of wealth.
125. Money is available to anyone who seeks it.
126. I attract others who share my wealth mindset and we support each other in creating unlimited abundance.
127. I am able to see opportunities where others see problems, which allows me to make money where others cannot.
128. I consciously remove any obstacles, physical or mental, to wealth and prosperity.
129. I consciously remove any obstacles, real or imagined, to wealth and prosperity.
130. I applaud the success of others and use it as inspiration for what is possible for me.
131. I think big and believe I can do anything I put my mind to.

132. I admire the successful and seek to emulate what they do to create my own success.
133. I put my money to work for me and have passive income assets that continually grow my fortune.
134. I respect those who are able to earn their own wealth and become rich.
135. I seek to be like those who are self-sufficient and create wealth on command.
136. Making money can be easy and doesn't have to be hard.
137. I am willing to put in the work to become rich, no matter how easy or hard it turns out to be.
138. I have a positive attitude about money and love it without shame.
139. Big life changes are opportunities to make big life changes.
140. When life brings change, it brings

with it an opportunity for me to grow in every way.

141. I love unexpected change because it forces me to increase in every area of my life.
142. Money is an amplifier—if I am sincere and good, I will only become more so.
143. Everyone has the right to become wealthy, myself included.
144. Money is not the root of all evil, it is the generator of all wealth.
145. My ability to generate wealth is without limit.
146. No matter how much wealth I generate, I always help others to become rich with me.
147. It is a human right to become wealthy, but only I can exercise that right.
148. Being rich, wealthy, and abundant is in alignment with my spiritual beliefs.

149. I owe it to my creator to become and achieve all that I can, making use of the gifts I have been given.
150. The are unlimited resources out there to help me become wealthy.
151. I will never stop my service to mankind and therefore will always receive wealth in return.
152. I will never stop loving humankind, and being generous with my wealth.
153. I am not ashamed of making money.
154. I do not need to shamefully hide my success, because it can serve as a motivator to others.
155. When people see my success, it opens their eyes to what is possible for them.
156. My mind is always focused on what positive things money can bring.
157. I do not love money for its own

sake, but for the positive things it can do for myself and others.

158. I am persistent and will overcome any obstacle that stands in the way of me and my financial future.

159. I am creative enough to always find quick, creative solutions to apparent problems in my business.

160. I will always do what it takes to gain success as long as it does not negatively affect my family and personal life.

161. All of my actions are in congruence with my financial goal of attaining wealth.

162. I believe in myself and in my own capacity to generate wealth and prosperity.

163. Those who envy me only fuel me even more towards my goals of success.

164. Those who doubt me only fuel me

even more towards my goals of success.

165. I follow the examples of others who are already living the life I want to live.
166. I accept the fact that those who are more wealthy must be providing more value.
167. The confidence I need to create wealth is already within me.
168. I am proud of the product or service I provide to others in exchange for money.
169. I don't make excuses when obstacles show up in my path towards my goals.
170. Other people's negativity does not deter me from reaching my goals.
171. What others perceive as limits on them has nothing to do with me.
172. I set my own personal possibilities, not the opinions of others.
173. As I master my ability to generate

wealth on command, I give back by teaching others what I know.
174. I love sharing knowledge and I love sharing wealth.
175. Money is the root of all prosperity.
176. I have a burning passion for growing my business.
177. The money I earn allows me to enjoy all the amazing things life has to offer.
178. Liberty is my most prized possession, and money is the most powerful way to preserve it.
179. I am dedicated to becoming all I can in life and in business.
180. I grow my money through wise investment decisions.
181. Time is the most precious commodity we all have, and time is money.
182. I gravitate towards those who are successful and admire the wealth and abundance they create.

183. Those who provide value to others deserve the money and success they receive in return.
184. Persistence pays off and I am a persistent person in pursuit of my goals.
185. I never give up when I am pursuing what is good and just.
186. Money obtained in the service of others is good and well-deserved.
187. I am willing to do the work required to change my family's financial future for the better.
188. Every day, I do something that gets me closer to achieving the success and abundance I desire.
189. I enjoy working when work it is in the service of others.
190. I enjoy earning money when I know it is in response to my service of others.
191. I deserve the rewards that come in

return of giving service and value to others.
192. I have definite clear plans that lead to my goal of generating wealth and abundance.
193. I fully commit to my plan to generate wealth and abundance.
194. I am full of great ideas that will result in wealth generation.
195. I pursue my good ideas so that they turn into money for me and value for others.
196. I am resourceful and always find answers to any questions I have.
197. I am resourceful enough to always be able to find a solution to any problem.
198. I am always able to seek and find the help I need when obstacles arise.
199. It is never too late to become rich or successful.
200. The attainment of wealth is

possible at any age, no matter how young or old.

201. Everywhere I look, I see opportunities conspiring to help me achieve my goals of success.
202. I see ways of making money all around me, all the time.
203. I am building an empire of wealth that will give me all the money I need and help me enrich the lives of others.
204. I am capable of generating all the money I will ever need.
205. I am creative, happy, and living in a world of unlimited abundance.
206. I effortlessly find money-making opportunities.
207. I am limitless and unstoppable when it comes to getting rich.
208. I am rich not just in finances, but also in my relationships.
209. I take action when I see an opportunity to make money.

210. I have what it takes to become rich.
211. I am thankful for the financial freedom that being wealthy brings.
212. I can bring freedom to myself and to others by generating unlimited amounts of wealth.
213. There is no glass ceiling when it comes to what I can achieve or how much money I can make.
214. My family and friends are happy to see me succeed.
215. I can have whatever I want whenever I want it.
216. I am always in the right place at the right time.
217. There is more money available than any of us can even imagine.
218. I am not just lucky — I deserve all the money I work to generate.
219. I attract more and more money with each passing year.

220. I am so happy to have met and exceeded my financial goals.
221. I look forward to getting a chance to share my abundance with others.
222. I am grateful to have more money than I know what to do with, and I will use it to provide greater service to humankind.
223. I can be whoever and whatever I want for the rest of my life.
224. I can do whatever I want for the rest of my life.
225. I can have whatever I want for the rest of my life.
226. I am a natural born success.
227. There is no such thing as luck — I earned everything I have.
228. I am destined to be rich.
229. I am destined to be wealthy.
230. I am destined to be successful.
231. Every day that goes by, I get richer and richer.

232. I am a powerful creative force, which is why it is easy for me to create wealth.
233. I share my talents and executed ideas with the world, and receive lots of money in return.
234. I have a clear idea of how much money I want to earn and what I am going to do to earn it.
235. I believe in my ability to make massive amounts of money.
236. I have the ability to create a million dollars over and over again.
237. Wealth is a mindset and I am wealthy inside and out.
238. Wealth outside comes from wealth within, and I have wealth within.
239. Money is a constantly renewing resource for me.
240. I am unified with wealth and prosperity.
241. My money is always multiplying.

242. I transform the lives of others with the money I attract into my life.
243. Money always flows into my life like a rushing river.
244. Wealth and prosperity are my birthright.
245. I was born rich on the inside, so I can easily get rich on the outside.
246. My external wealth is a reflection of my internal wealth.
247. I am willing to make whatever changes or improvements needed in myself to reach my financial goals.
248. It is fun to be rich and enjoy financial freedom.
249. My success breeds more success.
250. My wealth breeds more wealth.
251. My investments continually multiply, bringing me more money than I imagined.
252. I make money in my sleep with the power of my investments.

253. I make money in my sleep with the power of my passive income vehicles.
254. I am always discovering new ways to make more money.
255. I can manifest millions.
256. I am excited about generating millions of dollars in my life.
257. I love money and money loves me.
258. I am good and money is too.
259. I easily achieve my financial goals.
260. I always knew I would become rich.
261. I love money because money allows me to do what I love.
262. My bank accounts grow constantly without limit.
263. I am living my perfect life.
264. I am rich and confident.
265. I am prosperous and love helping others.
266. All of my businesses are successful.

267. Everything I touch turns to gold.
268. I attract successful people who work in harmony with me.
269. I am growing richer and richer and able to easily provide for my family.
270. I have enough wealth to take care of my family for the rest of their lives.
271. I love money because it allows me to fund the dreams of my loved ones.
272. Because I am rich, I decide what I do with my time.
273. I have unlimited amounts of wealth and can share it with others and generate even more wealth.
274. My choices are unlimited and I can help others without limit.
275. I enjoy being a multi-millionaire.
276. I allow myself to feel success and enjoy the fruits of my labor.

277. I feel like a success, I act like a success, I am a success.
278. I have no problems going out and claiming what is mine, and wealth is mine.
279. I expect prosperity and riches to flow to me.
280. As sure as the sun will rise, I will always be rich.
281. I joyously accept the money that flows into my life.
282. Money is only a tool that allows me to live the life of freedom that I want.
283. Success is my new normal.
284. Wealth is my new normal.
285. Abundance is my new normal.
286. I am amazed at how easily unlimited amounts of money come into my life.
287. I am attracted to money the way magnets are attracted to each other.

288. It was always my destiny to become rich.
289. Wealth generating ideas continually flow into my head.
290. Every success I enjoy generates a new success.
291. Every dollar I earn, turns into another.
292. Prosperity is my natural state of being.
293. I am a magnet for millions of dollars.
294. I deserve to make millions.
295. Rich people are good people, and I am both.
296. Wealth is nothing more than energy and I am continually drawing it towards me.
297. I can create a million dollars at will.
298. I am debt free and prosperous.
299. All of my needs are taken care of.
300. I can realize all my dreams.

301. Money is not just for others, it is for me.
302. I believe in my ability to make money multiply.
303. I enjoy the rewards I earn from the service I provide to others.
304. Success is all around me.
305. I am both happy and rich.
306. I am at peace with my wealth and my ability to maintain it.
307. I am at peace with my wealth and my ability to grow it.
308. My hard work pays off with financial rewards for me.
309. Earning money has always been easy for me.
310. Getting rich is a skill of mine.
311. Making money is easy when you provide value to others.
312. I alone am responsible for my relationship with money.
313. I alone am responsible for my attitude towards money.

314. My talents and persistence guarantee my success.
315. Abundance is a natural part of my life.
316. I can always generate the money that I need or want.
317. Money is my friend and it will help me and enable me to help others.
318. I am highly motivated in the pursuit of my financial goals.
319. I know that I will receive money in proportion to the value I provide others.
320. I do not always have to work for money, because my money works for me.
321. I am always attracting prosperous investment opportunities.
322. I am happy that I benefit financially from lucrative investments.

323. I am motivated to do a great job and get my work done on time.
324. Every action I take in my business is beneficial to its success.
325. I will always earn more than enough money than I need to survive.
326. The value I provide others translates into money that I deserve.
327. I have a lot to offer others and will be compensated in direct proportion to what I choose to provide.
328. I am deserving of the wealth I am constantly creating.
329. My talents are a gift to this world and I deserve the money they generate for me and my family.
330. My unique talents benefit those around me and help us all excel to the best of our abilities.
331. I trust in my ability to generate

money and prosperity and I will get it done.
332. I believe in my ability to keep going when things get tough.
333. I trust in my ability to amass wealth regardless of the political climate.
334. I trust in my ability to amass wealth no matter the state of the economy.
335. I bring in wealth from all corners of the world.
336. I am connected to the global economy and have customers all over the globe.
337. I trust myself to make wise and prosperous financial decisions.
338. Money always has and always will come naturally to me.
339. My mind is strong and helps me generate new ideas that attract money.
340. I don't earn money—I attract it in

direct proportion to the amount of value that I provide.

341. I refuse to let others place limits on the amount of money I can attain in my life.
342. There are no limits to the level to which I can monetize my talents.
343. There are no limits to the level to which I can monetize my ideas.
344. I have excellent intuition when it comes to knowing what to do with my money.
345. I have everything required to become a success.
346. Success, wealth, and financial prosperity are natural and my birthright.
347. I am proud of the money that I earn because I know I deserve it.
348. I am happy that I am rich because I believe I am worth it.
349. I am just as deserving as others are

of becoming wealthy and financially free.

350. I am always making money, whether I am actively working or not.
351. I am following the path toward more wealth and riches.
352. I can create any amount of money that anyone can name.
353. I easily learn new skills that help me earn more money.
354. I am intuitively pointed in the direction of wealth.
355. I am grateful to have the money to spend on things that enrich and improve my life.
356. I am always planting seeds that will help me earn more money in the future.
357. I love my work and the financial reward it brings.
358. I put my heart and soul into my

work and I am financially rewarded accordingly.

359. I take action each and every day that will increase my income.
360. I am grateful to have plenty of money to invest in my own mental health.
361. I am grateful to have plenty of money to invest in my own spiritual health.
362. I am grateful to have plenty of money to invest in my own physical health.
363. I love treating myself and the people I love with the money I have.
364. I love what money can do for me and love how it enables me to help others even more.
365. My wealth is constantly compounding over time.

Overcoming Limiting Beliefs

1. My fortune is already there, it is just waiting for me to go get it.
2. The universe is glorious and full of infinite love.
3. I am a naturally happy and successful person who is destined for a wonderful life.
4. I am capable of generating wealth just as much as anyone else.
5. I deserve to be rich just as much as anyone else.
6. Wealth is attracted to me and I can access it at any time.

7. I am open to new sources of wealth that the universe sends my way.
8. My wealth is ever increasing.
9. Things are always working out for me.
10. All situations in my business are working for my good.
11. I can increase my business bottom line to any number that I desire or choose.
12. Increasing my wealth just depends on me choosing to.
13. I can come up with wonderful ideas to increase my wealth.
14. There is always an opportunity to make more money.
15. I can make real what I see in my mind.
16. I can create the life I deserve and want with the skills that I currently have.
17. I can create the life I deserve and

want with the means that I currently have.
18. The only thing that could ever hold me back is myself.
19. Every difficulty is possible to overcome.
20. Nobody else controls my success but me.
21. I find it easy to make more money.
22. I can create anything and make it grow as large as I want.
23. The amount of money in the world is unlimited — I just have to attract it to me.
24. I find it easy to create new businesses and seize new opportunities.
25. I see joy, happiness, and abundance everywhere I go.
26. I accept the riches and money that freely and constantly come into my life.

27. Wealth often comes to me in unexpected ways.
28. I always earn more money than I thought possible.
29. My positive attitude draws money and abundance in my life.
30. I create wealth through positive thoughts in my mind.
31. I find it easy to meet my goals and this attracts more abundance.
32. I continuously attract money and use it to do good for myself and for others.
33. I give myself permission to be paid handsomely for the service I provide.
34. I can have anything I want because the universe is good and generous.
35. I magnetically attract prosperity.
36. An infinite amount of wealth already exists, and I am tapped into it.

37. I can draw wealth from the infinite supply of the universe.
38. Nobody can stop me from living up to my full potential.
39. I will be the best at my chosen career.
40. My life is easier because I can draw on an infinite supply of wealth.
41. Any company or project I create can become giant if I so choose.
42. There is no skill I can't master.
43. I choose to be wealthy and prosperous and to gain more wealth and prosperity every day.
44. There is an endless supply of money and I can have as much as I want.
45. I have a healthy attitude toward money and am happy with getting more of it.
46. I can advance as far in my career as I please.

47. I can travel anywhere I want.
48. I can learn any new skill I want to learn.
49. I can become anything there is to become in this world.
50. I am proud of others and happy for their success because I recognize that there is infinite wealth for everybody.
51. The success of others doesn't come at my expense.
52. We can all share in the universe's unlimited supply of wealth.
53. My background, age, race, and gender do not limit my capacity to create unlimited wealth.
54. There is an unlimited supply of customers who will pay me money for providing them value.
55. The product, services, and skills I provide are worth paying for and will rightly make me rich.
56. I approach learning with an

enthusiasm which helps me grow to new heights.
57. Every single day is an opportunity for new growth.
58. I have all the abilities I need to grow rich and successful.
59. I am intelligent and clever and there is no limit to how much more intelligent I can become.
60. I believe in myself and my abilities to get things done.

Cultivating Abundance In Thought & Reality

1. There is so much money available in the world that all of us can have whatever we want.
2. We live in a limitless universe that wants everyone to succeed.
3. There is a never ending flow of money coming into my life.
4. My success does not impede the success of others.
5. Other people's success does not impede my success.
6. There is more than enough for everyone.

7. The idea of competition is false because there is more than enough success to go around.
8. I am always receiving more money than I know what to do with.
9. My overflow of money allows me to live a life of prosperity, and I deserve it.
10. I take advantage of the many profitable opportunities that I see.
11. My business is always growing in strength and earning more money.
12. Growth for my business is inevitable.
13. The financial strength and longevity of my business is guaranteed.
14. There is uncapped potential for all of my business endeavors.
15. We could all be rich if we recognized the infinite wealth the universe provides.

16. It is always a good time for me to start a new business.
17. The abundance that is provided to me, I use to provide abundance to others.
18. I have ever renewing energy to put into my business and financial goals.
19. I live to give and do so often to share my prosperity with others.
20. My ability to generate wealth grows stronger every day.
21. I deserve to be paid well for the work I do because I do it to serve others.
22. I am enough.
23. I have a great mind for seeing all opportunities and turning them into money.
24. I attract money and well paying customers automatically.
25. I make a lot of money with calmness and ease.

26. I can create a new business easily and effortlessly.
27. Every business I create is successful and earns more profits than I could dream of.
28. I receive in abundance, and I also give in abundance.
29. I do more than what is expected of me, and therefore receive more that I expect in return.
30. I am overflowing with confidence.
31. I am brimming with success and possibility.
32. Money just comes to me whenever I ask for it.
33. There is an unending flow of ideas coming into my life.
34. I am full of passion for my work, which makes it easy for me to make more money.
35. No matter what I do, I rise to the top.

36. There is unstoppable greatness within me.
37. I embrace the massive success I have attained.
38. The game isn't rigged—and if it is, it is rigged in my favor.
39. I am in complete control of my fate.
40. All around me, are positive examples of wealth and generosity.
41. I give freely and joyfully, and I receive freely and joyfully.
42. My customer base is always growing with more and more quality clients.
43. I have a never ending flow of ideas on how to improve my business.
44. I can afford the best material things that life has to offer, and I deserve it all.
45. I can afford the best experiences that life has to offer, and I deserve it all.

46. I am rich because I choose to be rich.
47. I am a magnet for other success-oriented people.
48. I attract people into my life who are eager to seize opportunities.
49. I always have the choice to make more money rather than allowing others to control my life.
50. My network of wealthy friends is always expanding.
51. I am always surrounded by positive-minded action-takers.
52. My confidence overflows into others and inspires them to action.
53. I enjoy working and tapping into the unlimited supply of wealth that exists in the universe.
54. I am grateful for the infinite abundance the universe provides.
55. My life is full of unlimited wealth and abundance.

Success

1. I am an achiever in every area of life.
2. I am the kind of person who is always successful.
3. The more I have, the easier it is for me to get even more.
4. I have a passion for learning and growing, which attributes to my success.
5. I trust, know, and believe that my hard work always pays off.
6. I know that if I work hard, wealth,

prosperity, and abundance will be the result.
7. Each day, I discover new ways I can become more successful.
8. I believe in myself and my ability to generate wealth and success.
9. I can gain power and use it wisely to help others.
10. I will always leave the door open for new opportunities.
11. When I see an opportunity, I grab it so I can become more successful.
12. As long as I am on this earth, I am learning and putting in hard work for future rewards.
13. I will never stop growing my wealth and prosperity.
14. I look at the world through the eyes of an entrepreneur, so that I never miss an opportunity.
15. My growing prosperity opens new doors to greater opportunity.
16. I work hard now knowing that

there is unlimited success for me ahead.
17. I deserve wealth and abundance for the hard work I put in.
18. Everything that I try to do, I am able to excel in.
19. My relationships are just as full as my bank account.
20. I love the life that I am living.
21. I am blessed and successful beyond measure.
22. Seeing new opportunities is easy for me.
23. I create what I want when I want it.
24. I have a life that is balanced, whole, and amazing.
25. I am currently living my own personal definition of success.
26. I place no limits on what I can achieve and am willing to pay the price to get there.

27. I recognize that growth has a price and I am willing to pay it.
28. Abundance flows to me in unlimited amounts when I work hard to achieve it.
29. I can earn any amount of money I want by putting in the work.
30. I recognize opportunities and convert them into money and riches.
31. I am always on a quest for personal growth, which serves me in all areas of my life.
32. I move forward towards wealth without overthinking things.
33. I have a mind that is clear, alert, and focused, which helps me achieve success.
34. I have a well-rounded, successful life.
35. My mental peace is just as much an indicator of my success as my bank account.

36. Everything I do leads to more success for me.
37. I am proud of what I have achieved.
38. I can increase my streams of income whenever I so decide.
39. I multiply my success by working smarter, not harder.
40. We can all be wealthy if we work smart.
41. I always find a way to be successful no matter what.
42. My lifestyle is a reflection of the success I have attained.
43. Success is better when shared and I always find ways to share it.
44. I rejoice in the things I enjoy as a result of my work.
45. I spread happiness and joy and abundance.
46. Helping others is always an opportunity for success and creating a better life.

47. I have everything it takes to seize every opportunity.
48. Every business I create will flourish because I will do what it takes to ensure that.
49. I am swift to action, and my bank account reflects that.
50. I am living the life of my dreams.
51. I can afford anything I want because I have put in the work to build wealth.
52. I feel satisfied each day knowing I am working to secure my future.
53. Wealth and abundance are available in unlimited amounts for people like me who are willing to work for it.
54. I can build and create my dream home.
55. I can build and create my dream lifestyle.
56. I can build and create my dream life.

57. I am proud of the life that I have created for myself.
58. When I put in work, there is no limit to what I can achieve.
59. I grab opportunities and turn them into wealth magnets.
60. I am the kind of person who succeeds in everything I do.
61. I am comfortable with money and wealth because I've earned it.
62. In the end, hard work always pays off.
63. I can't lose because I do what it takes to win.

All by Drew McArthur on Amazon & Audible

Affirmations, Meditation, & Hypnosis For Positivity & A Success Mindset:

Power Of Thought To Create A Millionaire Mind, Manifest Wealth, Abundance, Better Relationships, & Form Positive Habits Now

Rewire Your Brain Affirmations, Meditation, & Hypnosis For Confidence, Motivation, & Discipline:

Increase Focus, Productivity, Willpower, Self Esteem, & Eliminate Distraction & Procrastination Habits

Step-By-Step Motivational Goal Setting Course For Life Mastery:

How To Change Your Brain, Set Your Vision, And Get Everything You Want To Have Your Best Year Ever

Monkey Mind Cure Affirmations, Meditation & Hypnosis:

How to Stop Worrying, Kill Fear, Rewire Your Brain, and Change Your Anxious Thoughts to Start Living a Stress and Anxiety-Free Life

Think Happy Thoughts: Affirmations and Meditation for Positive Thinking, Learned Optimism and A Happy Brain

Unlock the Advantage of the Happiness Habit and Project the Power of Positive Energy

Millionaire Money Mindset: Affirmations, Meditation, & Hypnosis

Using Positive Thinking Psychology to Train Your Mind to Grow Wealth, Think Like the New Rich and Take the Secret Fastlane to Success

www.ingramcontent.com/pod-product-compliance
Lightning Source LLC
Chambersburg PA
CBHW050322120526
44592CB00014B/2009